Girlology

[FASHION GURU]

Facts and Figures About Couture, Catwalks, and Cutting-Edge Trends

by Rebecca Rissman

CAPSTONE PRESS
a capstone imprint

Savvy Books are published by Capstone Press,
1710 Roe Crest Drive, North Mankato, Minnesota 56003
www.mycapstone.com

Library of Congress Cataloging-in-Publication Data
Names: Rissman, Rebecca, author.
Title: Fashion guru : facts and figures about couture, catwalks and
    cutting-edge trends / by Rebecca Rissman.
Description: North Mankato, Minnesota : Capstone Press, 2018. |
Series: Saavy. Girlology | Audience: Ages 9-13.
Identifiers: LCCN 2017046828 (print) | LCCN 2017047035 (ebook) |
ISBN 9781515778844 (ebook PDF) | ISBN 9781515778806 (hardcover)
Subjects: LCSH: Fashion—Juvenile literature.
Classification: LCC TT515 (ebook) | LCC TT515 .R57 2018 (print) | DDC
    746.9/2—dc23
LC record available at https://lccn.loc.gov/2017046828

Editorial Credits
Mandy Robbins, editor; Kayla Rossow and Charmaine Whitman, designers;
Kelli Lageson and Jo Miller, media researchers; Kathy McColley, production specialist

Printed and bound in the USA.
010846S18

TABLE OF CONTENTS

Chapter 1

THE WIDE WORLD OF FASHION

Fashion is where design meets function, and where self-expression combines — and often clashes — with comfort. Fashion is everything from new sneakers to a diamond-encrusted dress.

Famous designers have tried to explain what fashion is, but even these experts have struggled to capture the essence of the word.

"Fashion is architecture: it is a matter of proportions."

Designer Coco Chanel

"Fashion should be a form of escapism."

Designer Alexander McQueen

However it's defined, fashion can play a huge role in life. A look at the numbers of the fashion world can show just how much time, energy, and money people spend on what's in their closets.

A ROYAL WARDROBE

Queen Elizabeth was one of the first royal fashion icons in history. She used clothes, jewelry, and makeup to create an over-the-top image of a powerful queen. Her fashion sense influenced the people she ruled over.

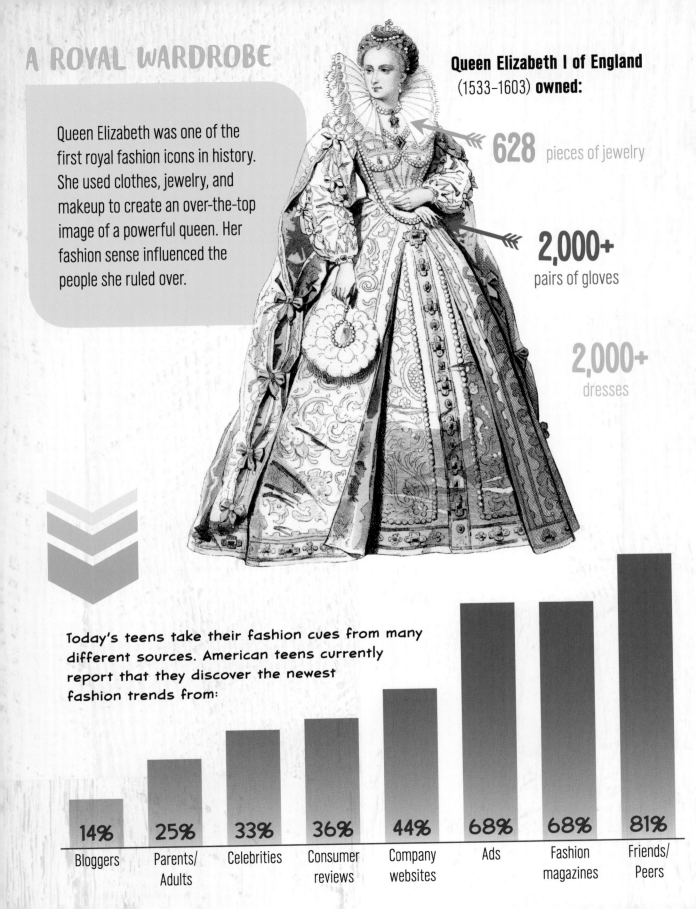

Queen Elizabeth I of England (1533–1603) **owned:**

628 pieces of jewelry

2,000+ pairs of gloves

2,000+ dresses

Today's teens take their fashion cues from many different sources. American teens currently report that they discover the newest fashion trends from:

Source	Percentage
Bloggers	14%
Parents/Adults	25%
Celebrities	33%
Consumer reviews	36%
Company websites	44%
Ads	68%
Fashion magazines	68%
Friends/Peers	81%

FASHION'S OUTRAGEOUS HISTORY

Humans have gone to great lengths to be fashionable for thousands of years. Let these numbers teach you a little of the far-out history of fashion.

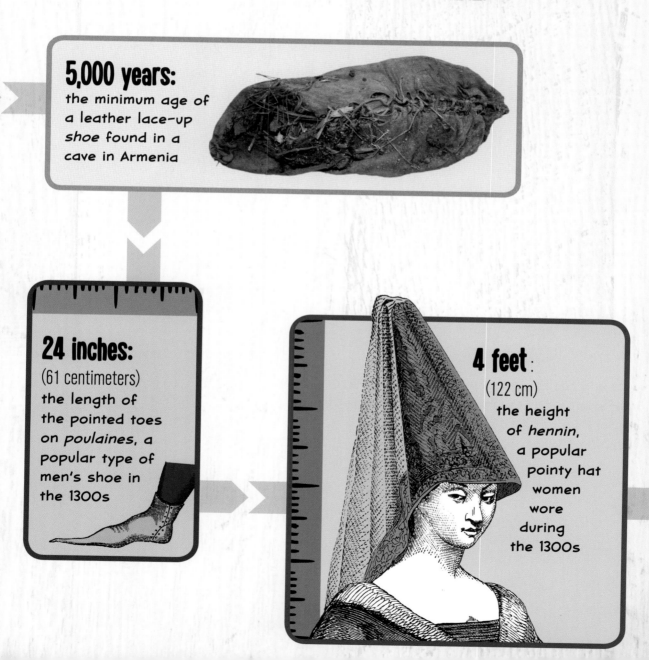

5,000 years:
the minimum age of a leather lace-up *shoe* found in a cave in Armenia

24 inches:
(61 centimeters) the length of the pointed toes on *poulaines*, a popular type of men's shoe in the 1300s

4 feet :
(122 cm) the height of *hennin*, a popular pointy hat women wore during the 1300s

30 inches:
(76.2 cm)
the height of some platform shoes, called *chopines*, in the 1400s

5 feet:
(152.4 cm)
the width of a woman's hips when she wore the popular bread-basket shaped *panniers* in the 1600s

3 feet:
(91.5 cm)
the height of Queen Marie Antoinette's favorite *Jolie Femme* wig

FASHION'S EVOLVING FINANCES

Many people think clothing is too expensive. But people actually spend less of their income on clothing than they did 100 years ago. Improvements in manufacturing and clothing technology have made clothing production cheaper and faster than ever before. As a result, prices have dropped.

Percentage of American income spent on clothes

14% 11.5% 3.3%

1901   1950   2015

In the past, people owned fewer clothing items. They made them last for years, often patching them or reusing the fabric for new garments.

Average price for a pair of shoes

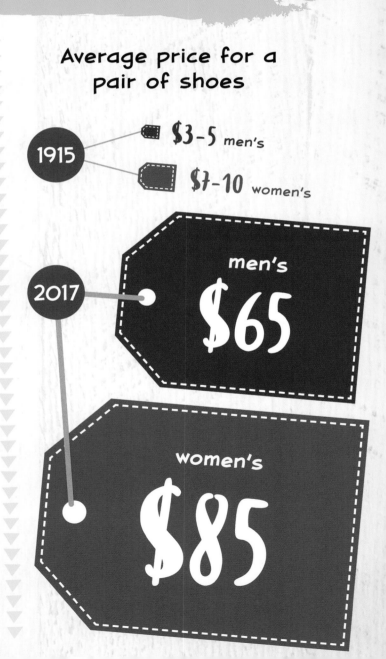

1915
$3–5 men's
$7–10 women's

2017
men's $65
women's $85

WORLD WAR II FASHIONS

During World War II (1939–1945), clothing and fabric was hard to come by. People were limited in what they could buy. They were encouraged to get creative with clothing. People repaired, recut, and repurposed unique items to stay fashionable. American bride Rosalie Bourlund was one of many wartime brides who took this message to heart. She used the parachute that saved her fiance's life as fabric for her wedding gown.

Go through your wardrobe

Make-do and Mend

MAKING DO

During the war, clothing in Britain was rationed. The government sent out a pamphlet called "Make Do and Mend." It gave women ideas on how to stretch their current wardrobes. Tips included:

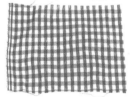
Add decorative patches to cover holes in worn-out clothing.

Unravel sweaters to use the yarn for knitting new clothing.

Use old clothing and even men's clothing as fabric to sew new outfits.

SIZE WISE

Clothing manufacturers make garments in different sizes. This helps customers choose items that will fit. Clothing sizes can make shopping fast and easy. However, not all clothing sizes match up. In fact, very few do!

1800–1820s
The first standardized clothing sizes appear. They are primarily for men's military uniforms.

1920s–1930s
Plus size clothing appears in the United States and the United Kingdom.

1958
"True Sizing" first appears. It is a standardized set of numbers used for women's clothing sizes.

1999
Designer Nicole Miller creates the first ever size 0 garment.

Over time, clothing sizes have reflected a population that is getting bigger. This means that bigger people wear smaller sizes now than they did in the past.

12
The size Marilyn Monroe wore in the 1950s

The size she would wear today
6

ONE SIZE FITS ALL?

Different designers use different measurements for their sizing. This means that an 8 in one label will be a different size in another. Experts estimate that the following designer size 8s actually match up with the following average sizes:

Size 8 •	Dior	Marc Jacobs and **Theory**	[average size]	Gap	Old Navy and **Target**

Actual Size:	4	6	8	10	12

SIZES AROUND THE WORLD

Sizes don't just differ between designers. Different countries often use entirely different sizing systems. The same dress would be sized in different ways in different countries.

7 US

6/8 UK

40 Italy

34 Scandinavia, Germany

170 China

8 Australia

36 France, Spain, Portugal

7–9 Japan

Chapter 2

FASHION STAPLES

IF THE SHOE FITS

Shoes are a necessity, but they're also style statements.
The average American's shoe buying habits differ by gender.
But the number of shoes they regularly wear is about the same.

Average pairs of shoes...

owned by
American men: **12**

owned by
American women: **27**

regularly worn by
most Americans: **3-4**

= 1 pair

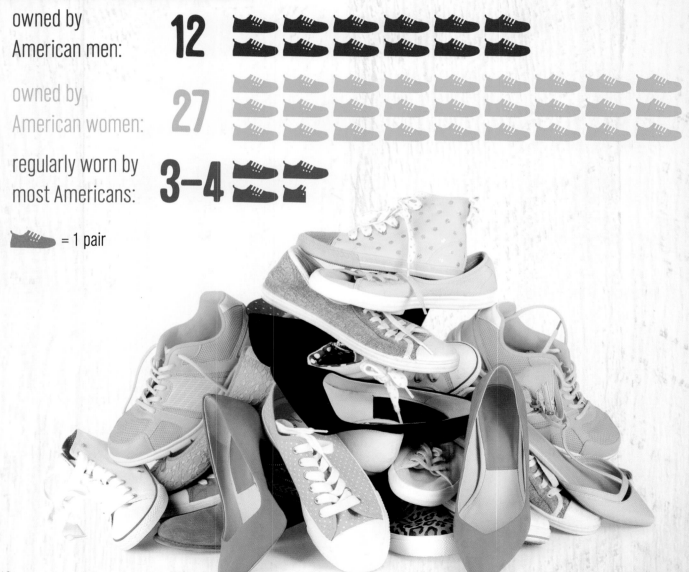

GREAT HEIGHTS

High heels can make quite the fashion statement, especially when they are very, very high. But some heels get a bit out of control. Check out some of the craziest heels in recent history.

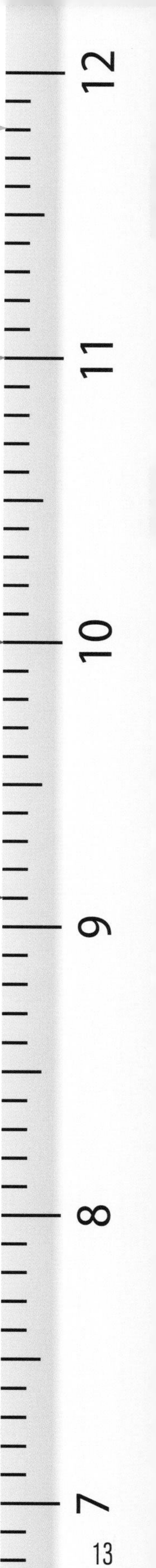

11.8 inches
Alexander McQueen's "Armadillos"

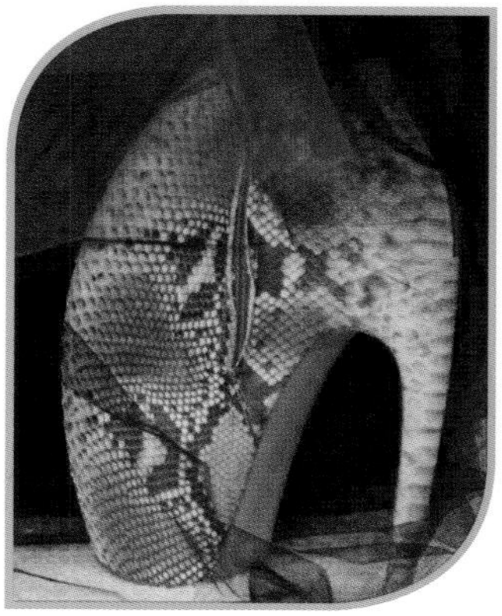

11 inches
Nina Ricci heelless shoes

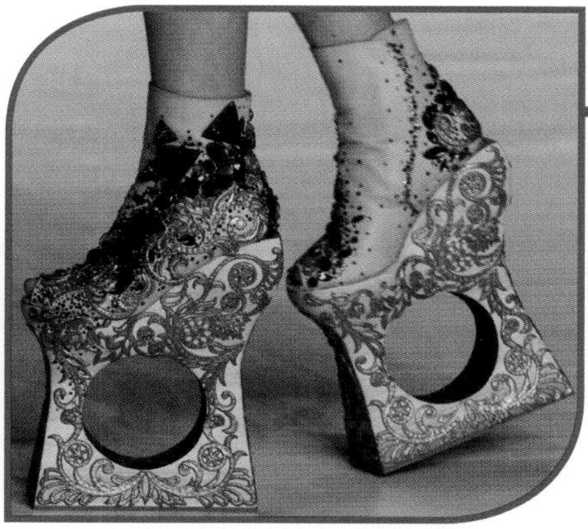

10 inches
Guo Pei's "Geisha Platforms"

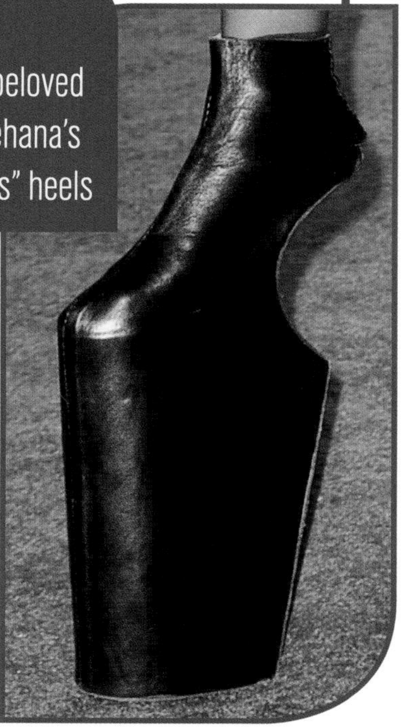

9.1 inches
Lady Gaga's beloved Noritaka Tatehana's "Night Makers" heels

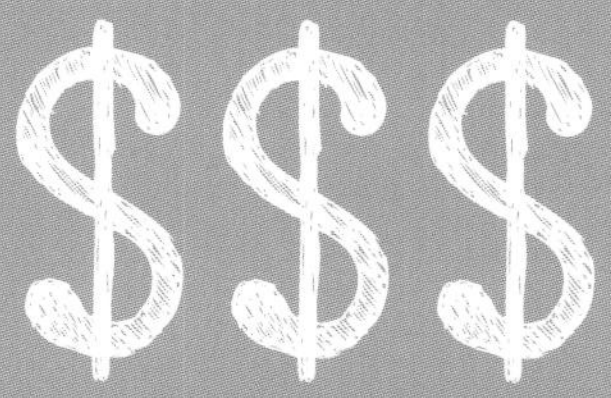

Do you love buying shoes? Calculating how long you need to work to buy a pair of shoes is a good way to decide whether a new pair is worth it!

6 hours
Average amount of time an American must work to buy one pair of shoes

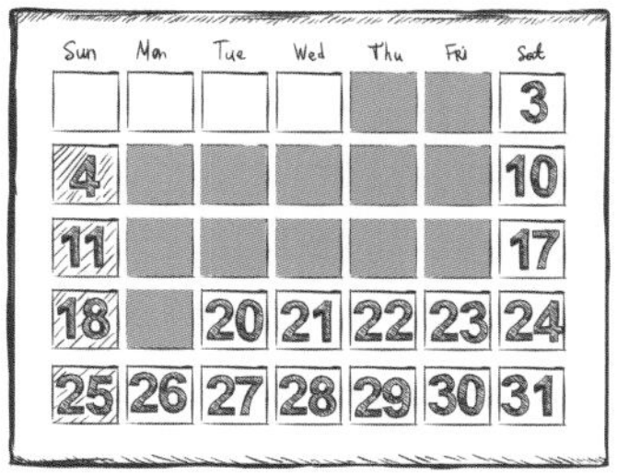

2 1/2 weeks
Average amount of time it takes Americans to earn what they spend on shoes each year

NUMBERS UNDERNEATH

Some people call them "drawers." Other people call them "undies." Underwear can go by many names. No matter what they're called, undergarments are important. They help keep clothing clean, comfortable, and well-fitting.

Some people prefer a full drawer of drawers.

The average number of pairs of underwear British women own: **34**

Women who fold their underwear: **56%**

Men's underwear facts can be very revealing too.

7 the number of years the average man in the U.S. and U.K. keeps each pair of underwear

1935 the year men's briefs were invented

0 the recommended number of undergarments worn under a Scottish kilt

Royal Fantasy Bra

SPENDY UNDIES

Most bras are fairly inexpensive. However, retail brand Victoria's Secret has a tradition of creating expensive fantasy bras decorated with precious jewels for their fashion shows. Here are some of their priciest bras.

$15 million
The price of the Red Hot Fantasy Bra, worn by Gisele Bundchen in 2000

$12.5 million
The price of the Heavenly Star Bra, worn by Heidi Klum in 2001

$10 million
The price of the Royal Fantasy Bra, worn by Candice Swanepoel in 2013

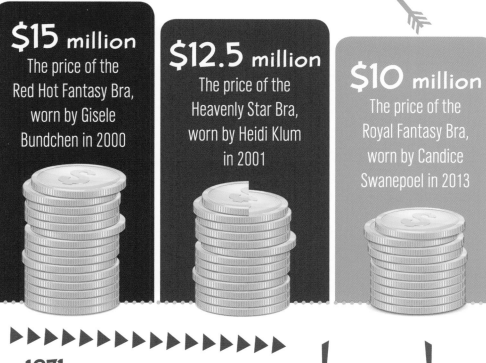

▶▶▶▶▶▶▶▶▶▶▶▶▶▶▶▶▶

1871
The year famous author Mark Twain invented the clasp used on most bras

▶▶▶▶▶▶▶▶▶▶▶▶▶▶▶▶

ADDING UP ACCESSORIES

Whether it's a tasteful pair of earrings or a gigantic gold chain, fashionistas know that the right accessories can make or break an outfit. Necklaces, bracelets, earrings, rings, and other accessories can help personalize every ensemble.

WHAT A WATCH!

Wrist watches aren't just stylish accessories. They are also useful. One high-end Swiss watchmaker has managed to cram hundreds of amazing functions into one small timepiece, called the Grande Sonnerie.

935 The number of parts inside the Grande Sonnerie

$1.15 million The price for one Grande Sonnerie watch

5–8 The number of Grande Sonnerie watches created each year

11 years The time it took to develop the technology needed for the Grande Sonnerie

= 10 parts

CELEBRITY ENGAGEMENT RINGS, BY THE NUMBERS

Some of the most admired accessories adorn ladies' left ring fingers. Engagement rings offer a sparkle that's hard to miss – especially on some celebrities.

A carat is a weight measurement for how large a gemstone is. The average engaged or married American woman sports a 1-carat center stone in her engagement ring.

4.00 ct	3.00 ct	2.00 ct	1.75ct	1.50 ct	1.25 ct
1.00 ct	0.75 ct	0.50 ct	0.25 ct	0.10 ct	0.05 ct

Carats	What
1	average American woman's gem
12	Kate Middleton's sapphire
20	Kim Kardashian West's diamond
33.19	film icon Elizabeth Taylor's diamond
40	former first lady Jacqueline Kennedy Onassis' diamond

Chapter 3

THE FASHION INDUSTRY

The fashion industry is booming with opportunities, especially for women.

60–75 million people work in the apparel industry. This number includes everyone from the factory workers who make fabrics to fashion designers who create-one-of-a-kind outfits.

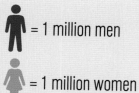

75% of garment workers are **women**.

= 1 million men

= 1 million women

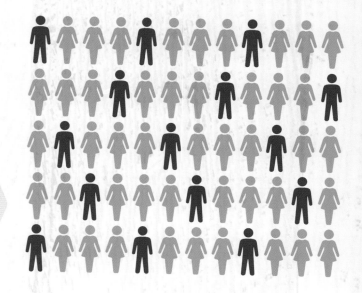

Some fashion workers earn heaps of cash, while others struggle to get by.

per year

$306,600: Chief Marketing Officer in the U.S.

$191,000: Creative Director in the U.S.

$187,000: Marketing Manager in the U.S.

$60,000: Fashion retail store manager in the U.S.

$24,000: Fashion retail store worker in the U.S.

$1,836: Garment factory worker in Cambodia

CONCEPT TO CLOSET

Every new fashion item starts as an idea. Then it takes a long, winding journey until it lands in someone's closet!

Fashion designer thinks of an idea.

Designer sketches a jacket.

Seamstress mocks it up.

Jacket is sewn.

Individual stores determine the quantity of the jacket they want.

Fashion buyers select the jacket for their stores.

Designer features jacket in a fashion show.

Jacket is shipped to stores.

Jacket is purchased by consumer.

Jacket winds up in closet.

COST OF U.S. IMPORTS

The United States fashion industry imports much of the cloth and other materials it uses from other countries. This chart shows how much money U.S. companies spend on fashion goods from a few countries.

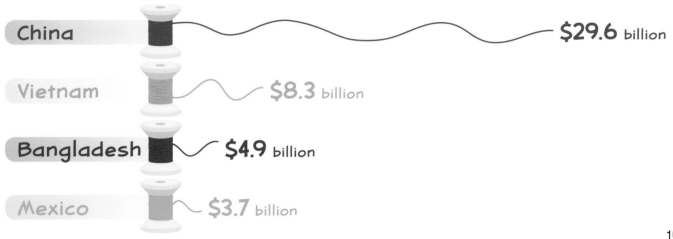

China — **$29.6** billion

Vietnam — **$8.3** billion

Bangladesh — **$4.9** billion

Mexico — **$3.7** billion

ALL IN A DAY'S WORK

It might seem like the only people who work in fashion are models, designers, and photographers. But the fashion industry employs all types of people working in a variety of careers.

◄◄◄◄◄◄◄◄◄◄◄◄◄◄◄◄◄◄◄◄

A fashion design house relies on a wide range of skilled employees to churn out the hottest styles season after season. Common departments within fashion houses include sales and marketing, design and creative, product and supply, finance, and human resources.

◄◄◄◄◄◄◄◄◄◄◄◄◄◄◄◄◄◄◄◄

FASHION DEPARTMENTS

Marc Jacobs is an American fashion designer who employs about 1,300 people. This chart shows the company's makeup.

Sales & Marketing **31%**

Design & Creative **16%**

Operations, ... **9%**
including product & supply

.... **3%**

.... 2%

Finance ....

Human Resources ....

Other **36%**

ENORMOUS EMPLOYERS

The following fashion giants employ huge numbers of people:

Moët Hennessy Louis Vuitton
134,000 people

Christian Dior
140,000 people

Gap
150,000 people

Zara
152,000 people

- 150,000
- 140,000
- 130,000
- 120,000
- 110,000
- 100,000

GLOBAL GARMENT WORKER EARNINGS

In very poor parts of the world, some people employed as garment workers earn very little. They are usually paid by the hour.

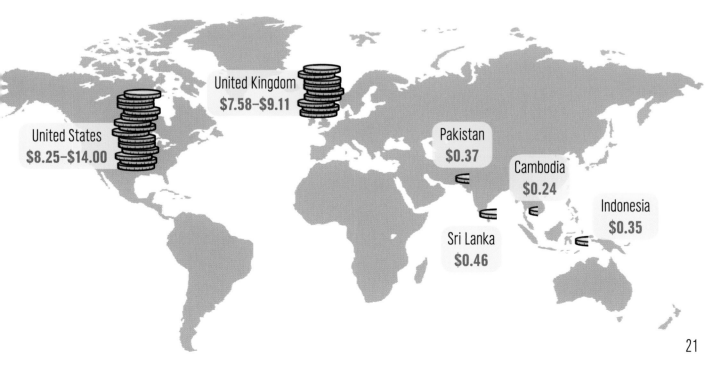

United Kingdom
$7.58–$9.11

United States
$8.25–$14.00

Pakistan
$0.37

Cambodia
$0.24

Indonesia
$0.35

Sri Lanka
$0.46

21

THE GEOGRAPHY OF FASHION

Many people associate fashion with cities such as Paris, France, or New York City. But fashion is a global industry, dependent on people from all over the planet.

Leading producers of		
Cotton ⬤	**Silk** ⬤	**Wool** ⬤
United States	China	United States
Uzbekistan	India	Australia
China	Uzbekistan	New Zealand
India		

GLOBE-TROTTING TEE

A single T-shirt can take a worldwide journey.

1 Farmers grow cotton in the United States.

2 Factory workers spin cotton into yarn in Indonesia.

3 Yarn is shipped to Bangladesh where workers spin it into fabric.

4 Workers in Colombia sew the fabric into a shirt.

5 Shirt is sent to a shipping facility in New York City.

6 The shipping workers send the shirt to a store in Anchorage, Alaska.

7 Consumer buys shirt.

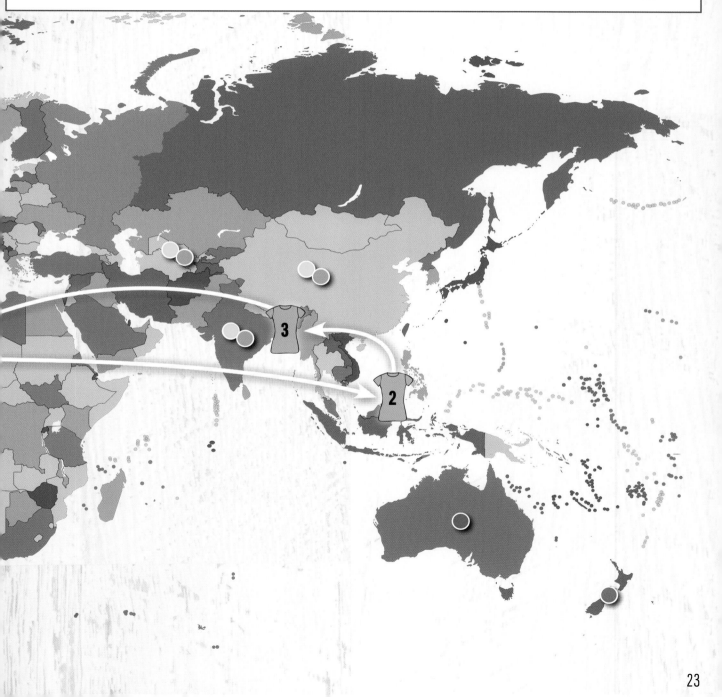

FASHION AND THE ENVIRONMENT

Fashion has a big impact on the world, and not just in terms of style. The apparel industry is one of the biggest energy consumers on the planet. This means that fashion production can contribute to problems such as global warming.

10% of the world's carbon footprint comes from clothing production.

A carbon footprint describes the harmful gases that contribute to global warming.

Creating some fashions can produce enormous amounts of harmful gases.

  **20 miles** Manufacturing one t-shirt produces the same amount of carbon dioxide as driving this far.

78 miles Manufacturing one pair of jeans produces the same amount of carbon dioxide as driving a truck this far.

WHERE DOES IT GO?

Unwanted clothing can pile up fast. Unfortunately, most of it ends up burned or in landfills. Donating your old clothes to thrift shops or selling it secondhand can help.

Where did unwanted clothes in the U.S. end up in 2014?

85% went to a landfill or incinerator.

15% was donated to charity or thrift stores.

Of the donations...

Up to **75%** are resold

The rest are sent to outlet stores or packaged and sent overseas for resale.

GARB IN THE GARBAGE

Many people simply throw their old clothing into the trash.

5 tons The amount of old clothes one New York City charity received each day in 2012

80 lbs The amount of clothes each American throws away every year

1.5 million tons The amount of clothes and textiles British people toss into landfills per year

Chapter 4

TRENDING FIGURES

Fashion trends fade in and out of popularity. Bell bottom pants were a big trend in the 1970s. Bomber jackets were hot in the 1980s. Baby doll dresses were a hit in the 1990s.

Fashion designers are often behind the rise and fall of trends. But most designers encourage people not to invest too much in trends.

TREND TRAILS

Fashion trends start in different places. Some begin in a designer's studio. Others start on the street.

"Don't be into trends. Don't make fashion own you, but you decide what you are, what you want to express by the way you dress and the way you live."

Gianni Versace

One Trail

Street style → Instagram post → Celebrity endorsement → Fashion designers respond.

Another Trail

Fashion designer creation → Fashion show → Retail item → Consumer

HELLO, OLD FRIEND

Many trends and popular brands don't appear just once.
Some enjoy multiple waves of popularity.

20 years: Typical time it takes for a trend to reemerge

1960s	Skinny jeans are a hot new trend.
1970	Bell bottoms take over as the top pants style.
1980s	Skinny jeans are popular again.
1990	Bell bottoms are a hot trend again.
1990	Neon colors become the look to have.
1995	Chunky becomes the hottest look in footwear.
1997	Flannel shirts are the top look in tops.
2010s	Skinny jeans come back into style.
2010	Neon becomes hot again.
2015	Chunky work boots are popular again.
2017	Flannel shirts are back on trend.

DELIGHTFUL DENIM

Blue jeans are a nearly world-wide fashion phenomenon. With the exception of a few remote corners of the world, jeans can be spotted just about anywhere.

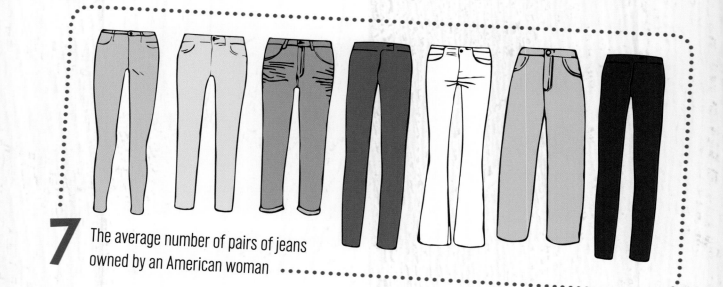

7
The average number of pairs of jeans owned by an American woman

WHEN TO WASH

While many people agree that blue jeans are great, some argue about how best to care for them.

Every 3-6 wears
...How often most Americans wash their jeans

Experts recommend you wash your denim... **every 6 months.**

NEVER
This is how often Levi Strauss' CEO recommends people wash their jeans in a washing machine. If your jeans get dirty, he recommends that you carefully spot clean them.

A DENIM TIMELINE

Jeans weren't always so popular. They actually began as sturdy work pants for laborers in the American West. Over time, celebrities helped popularize them, and they became a garment seen almost everywhere.

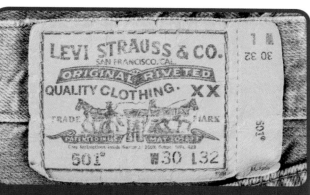

John Wayne wears Levi's XX jeans, now called 501s, in the film *Stagecoach*.

1873 Levi Strauss and tailor Jacob Davis patent their "XX" pants. These work pants were unique because they had little metal rivets sewn into the corners of the pockets to reinforce them. Tags on Levi's today reference the company's origins.

1939

1940s American soldiers wear blue jeans abroad, making them more popular.

1954 Marilyn Monroe wears blue jeans in *River of No Return*.

1967 The band Jefferson Airplane plays in a mind-bending radio ad for white Levis.

1970 The Ramones wore ripped Levis on the cover of their album "Rocket to Russia."

1979

1980s Baggy jeans become a popular look in hip-hop fashion.

2001 Britney Spears and Justin Timberlake show up at the AMAs in all denim.

2009 President Barack Obama throws out the opening pitch at the MLB All-Star game in unfashionable jeans that the media soon nicknames his "dad jeans."

2017 Christian Ronaldo, the world's highest paid athlete, launches his own denim line called CR7 Denim.

Super short "Daisy Dukes" denim shorts appear on the TV show *Dukes of Hazzard*.

HAIRSTYLES COUNT

Whether it's long, short, spiky, curly, or rainbow colored, hair is a fabulous part of any fashion statement.

COST OF A CUT

The price of a haircut can vary a great deal. Here's a look at the average cost of a woman's haircut in a few countries:

18 feet, 5 inches The longest hair in the world, belonging to Xie Quiping

1948 The year hairspray was invented

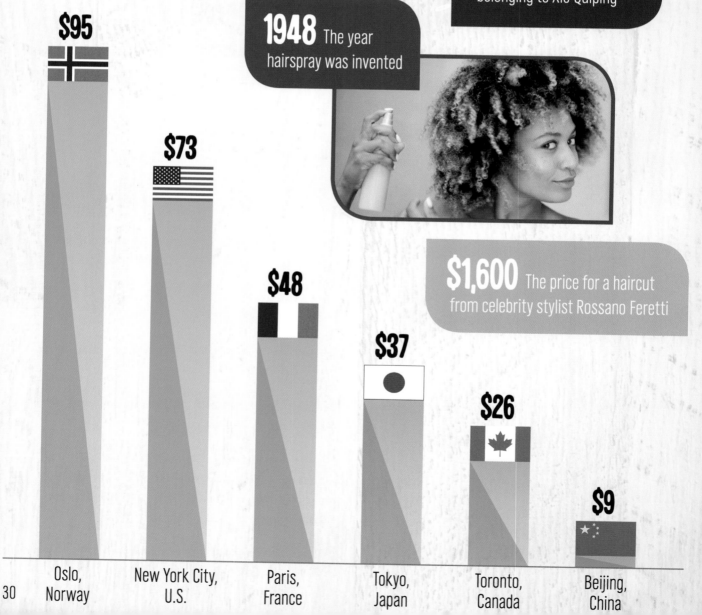

$1,600 The price for a haircut from celebrity stylist Rossano Feretti

$95 — Oslo, Norway

$73 — New York City, U.S.

$48 — Paris, France

$37 — Tokyo, Japan

$26 — Toronto, Canada

$9 — Beijing, China

A MANE OF MANY COLORS

Rainbow hair is a popular trend that involves bleaching all the natural color out of hair, then dying it many different bright colors. The process isn't easy, or cheap. But rainbow fashion fans say it's worth it!

$ 200-1,000
The cost at a salon for rainbow hair

3-8 hours
The time it takes in a hair salon to achieve this look

every 4-6 weeks
How often the hair needs to be re-dyed to maintain its color

IT ALL ADDS UP: FASHION AND SHOPPING

American teenagers' spending habits reveal that fashion is a high priority.

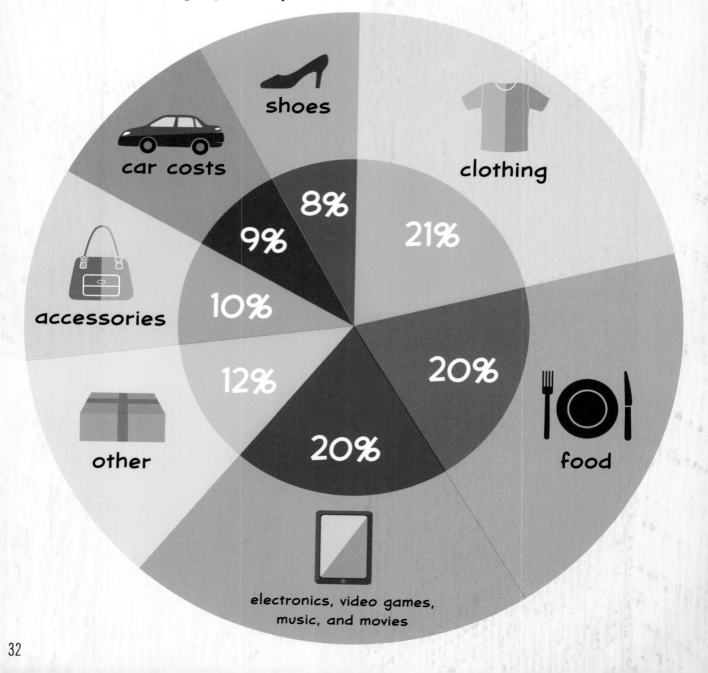

shoes — 8%

car costs — 9%

accessories — 10%

other — 12%

clothing — 21%

food — 20%

electronics, video games, music, and movies — 20%

PROM PREP

Shopping for the right outfit for school dances, such as prom, can be expensive. *Seventeen Magazine* conducted a poll and discovered that its readers spent the following amount on their perfect prom looks:

$231	dress
$45	shoes
$23	handbag
$50	hair
$68	nails and makeup
$32	jewelry
$449	TOTAL

Online shopping is a growing phenomenon. More and more consumers are turning to the internet for their fashion fix.

79% of Americans shop online.

55% of online shoppers buy clothing or other apparel.

24% of Cyber Monday and Black Friday sales purchases were clothing.

Chapter 5

THE MODELING WORLD

MODELING MOOLAH

They strut, they pose, and they pout. But do models cash in? The financial figures behind these fashionable figures tell an interesting tale. Some jobs pay much more than others.

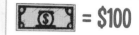 = $100

$150 per day — The amount models are paid for editorial work, such as magazines

$2,500 per day — The amount models are paid for commercial work, such as advertisements

TOP 10 MODEL PRODUCERS

Many models come from the same areas of the world. Here are the top 10 model-producing nations:

1 Estonia
2 Iceland
3 Lithuania
4 Denmark
5 Latvia
6 Sweden
7 Netherlands
8 Slovakia
9 Norway
10 Czech Republic

Many modeling careers start early, and they don't last long!

16
Age most models begin working

5 years
Average length of a modeling career

FAMOUS FACES

Only the very best models make it onto the cover of *Vogue* magazine. Some have been lucky enough to do it many times!

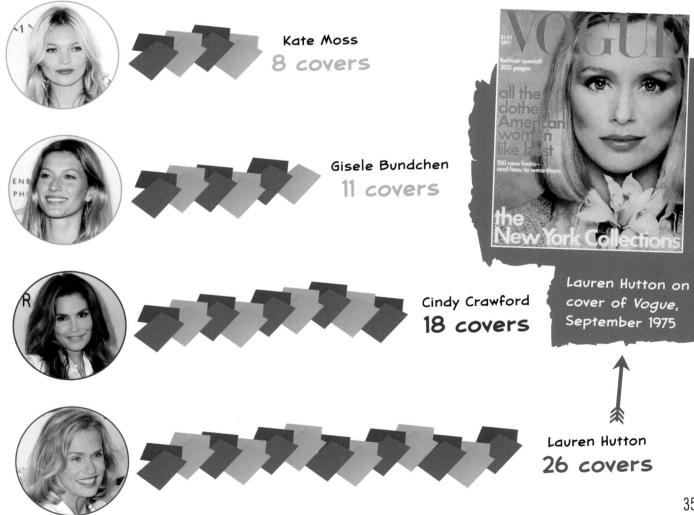

Kate Moss
8 covers

Gisele Bundchen
11 covers

Cindy Crawford
18 covers

Lauren Hutton on cover of *Vogue*, September 1975

Lauren Hutton
26 covers

THE CATWALK COUNTS AT NEW YORK FASHION WEEK

Fashion shows showcase designers' latest creations. Major shows attract celebrities. Some of the most famous shows of all happen during New York Fashion Week (NYFW).

The seating charts at a fashion show are very important. Department store fashion buyers, wealthy fashion fans, socialites, journalists, and celebrities are all vying for the best seats.

CATWALK

Front row: fashion bloggers, magazine editors, celebrities, socialites

Second row: fashion writers, fashion buyers, journalists, other fashion personalities

Third row: other journalists, friends of the designer, people involved in fashion business decisions

1943 The year New York Fashion Week first occurred

270+ Designer shows during NYFW

5–6 Number of runway shows top models might walk in per day

7–20 minutes Average length of a fashion runway show

31.6 million Number of times the hashtag #NYFW was used in 2015

32 the number of cans of hairspray one stylist used for the models in a single NYFW show

$460,000 Average amount a single runway show costs to produce

$100,000 Amount some designers pay celebrities to attend their shows

2,000 The number of bottles of nail polish one celebrity nail artist and her team goes through during NYFW

NUMBERS OF NOTE: HAUTE COUTURE

Haute couture is the term used to describe a very luxurious type of high fashion. "Haute couture" means that something is handmade from start to finish, using only the best materials.

2 The minimum number of fashion shows haute couture houses must produce each year

15 The number of official haute couture fashion houses in France today

2,200 The number of haute couture seamstresses employed today

35 The number of "looks," or outfits, required for each fashion show

= 100 seamstresses

TONS OF TIME

Haute couture garments are often intricate and take a very long time to create. To wrap your brain around just how long the process is, take a look at it in days. If seamstresses worked around the clock with no breaks for food or sleeping, it would look something like this:

1,000 hours=41.7 days

The time it may take to create a couture gown with embroidery or special features

S	M	T	W	T	F	S
1	2	3	4	5	6	7
8	9	10	11	12	13	14
15	16	17	18	19	20	21
22	23	24	25	26	27	28
29	30	31				

S	M	T	W	T	F	S
			1	2	3	4
5	6	7	8	9	10	11
12	13	14	15	16	17	18
19	20	21	22	23	24	25
26	27	28	29	30		

200 hours=8.3 days

The time it may take to create a simple couture outfit

S	M	T	W	T	F	S
1	2	3	4	5	6	7
8	9	10	11	12	13	14

$200,000+

The cost of a haute couture evening gown

$ = $1,000

10 The maximum number of any particular haute couture design that may be created

39

Chapter 6

FASHION IN THE MEDIA

The Academy Awards, or Oscars, don't just celebrate film. They also display fashion. Stars walk the red carpet wearing jaw-dropping styles.

COST OF AN OSCARS LOOK

Hair	$1,500–$4,000
Makeup	$1,500–$4,000
Gown	Most actresses borrow them from designers for free, though they are worth anywhere from **$15,000–$100,000**.
Jewelry	**$1 million–$18 million** Like dresses, jewelry is often borrowed from designers.
Shoes	**$1,000**
Stylist	**$10,500** Cost of a celebrity stylist to put the whole look together

Gowns, shoes, jewelry, hair, and makeup can get spendy for Oscars attendees. Luckily, many film studios foot the bill for award show fashions!

PHOTO FRENZY

The Oscars Red Carpet is big business for photographers hoping to get a great shot.

4,085 The number of photos one red carpet photographer can expect to take

= 100 photos

40% of red carpet photographers are women.

60% of red carpet photographers are men.

STAR STEALS

Not everything on the red carpet is horribly expensive. Some stars sported budget friendly items at the 2017 Oscars.

$10

Nicole Kidman's lip gloss

$54

Diane Kruger's purse

$160

Halle Berry's high heels

STYLE ON THE SILVER SCREEN

Style-savvy viewers around the world love to tune in to watch fashion television. Design competitions and fashion-focused reality television provide entertainment and style inspiration at the same time.

RUNWAY TIMELINE

Project Runway is a television sensation that has come a long way from the show's humble roots.

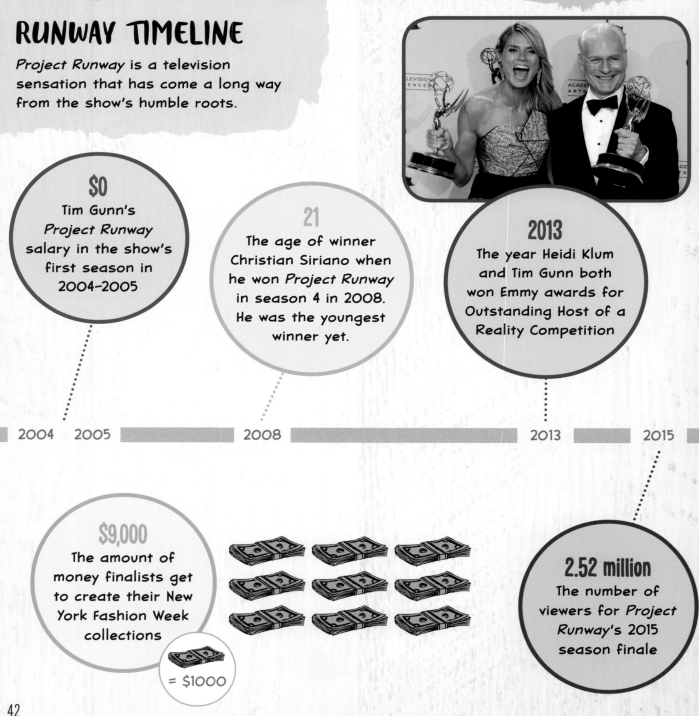

$0
Tim Gunn's *Project Runway* salary in the show's first season in 2004–2005

21
The age of winner Christian Siriano when he won *Project Runway* in season 4 in 2008. He was the youngest winner yet.

2013
The year Heidi Klum and Tim Gunn both won Emmy awards for Outstanding Host of a Reality Competition

2004   2005   2008   2013   2015

$9,000
The amount of money finalists get to create their New York Fashion Week collections

= $1000

2.52 million
The number of viewers for *Project Runway's* 2015 season finale

SPIN-OFF STATS

Project Runway: Junior is a spinoff of *Project Runway* aimed at younger viewers.

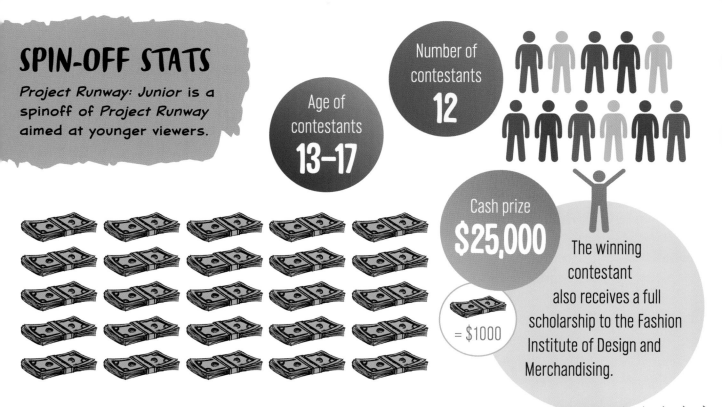

Age of contestants
13–17

Number of contestants
12

Cash prize
$25,000

= $1000

The winning contestant also receives a full scholarship to the Fashion Institute of Design and Merchandising.

MODELS IN THE MAKING

America's Next Top Model documents a heated contest for aspiring fashion models.

23 The number of seasons of *ANTM* competitions

150 The number of countries that air *ANTM*

SOCIAL MEDIA COUNTS IN THE FASHION WORLD

Today, even the highest levels of fashion can be influenced by a tweet, blog, or Instagram post. This means that one of the most important tools in the fashion world may just be the smartphone in your back pocket.

HELPFUL HASHTAGS

Hashtags make posts on social media easy to find. Here are some of 2016's top fashion hashtags:

1 #ootd (Outfit of the Day)

2 #instafashion

3 #vintage

4 #fashionblogger

5 #fashionista

CAREER CASH

$5,000–$25,000	Price some brands will pay top names for an Instagram post featuring their products
$1 million–$3 million	Annual salary of top fashion Instagrammers

STYLE INFLUENCERS

Some social media stylists have an enormous influence.

The Blonde Salad

1.2 million Facebook likes

398 thousand Instagram followers

Chiara Ferragni

Wendy Nguyen

Wendy's Lookbook

661,985 YouTube subscribers

40 million Views for her "How to Tie a Scarf" video

Chapter 7
FASHION'S BRIGHT FUTURE

Fashion is constantly evolving. Today, designers are pioneering ways to combine technology with apparel. Their discoveries will ensure that the closets of tomorrow are stylish and smart.

SOLAR POWER

Tommy Hilfiger is pushing the limits of wearable technology. In 2014 the clothing label released solar-powered jackets that can charge electronic devices. The jackets were fitted with water resistent panels. The panels were connected to a battery pack in one of the front pockets. Connected to the battery was a double USB port, which let the wearer charge two devices at once.

Retail
$599

Half of the proceeds from the sales of the jackets went to the Fresh Air Fund. This non-profit organization provides outdoor camps and summer adventures for low-income, inner-city youth.

SPENDY STYLES

Some futuristic fashions are very expensive.

$300
approximate cost of a Hug shirt

A Hug shirt allows people to use their phones to send hugs digitally to friends. When a friend sends a hug, the person wearing the shirt will feel it give them a "hug."

$1,599
cost of light-up bra, fitted with tiny LEDs

$564–$600
3-D printed shirt

SMART STATS

6 million
Reported number of people who bought Apple watches in the last three months of 2016, according to Apple

17% of people now own smartwatches or fitness trackers.

$350–$17,000
The range of prices for Apple watches

$ = $1,000

$ $ $ $ $ $ $ $ $ $ $ $ $ $ $ $ $

Author Bio

Rebecca Rissman is an award-winning children's author. Her writing has been praised by *School Library Journal*, *Booklist*, *Creative Child Magazine*, and *Learning Magazine*. She has written more than 200 books about history, science, art, and culture. Rissman is especially interested in fashion and the way it intersects with culture. She has authored several books about the history of fashion, female fashion designers and influencers, and fashion trends. Rissman lives in Chicago, Illinois, with her husband and two daughters.

Books in This Set